D1202348

THE BEST OF TIMES...

Peter Brookes

BOOKS

First published in Great Britain in 2009 by
JR Books, 10 Greenland Street, London NW1 0ND
www.jrbooks.com

Copyright © 2009 Peter Brookes and Times Newspapers, Ltd

Peter Brookes has asserted his moral right to be identified as the Author of this Work in accordance with the Copyright Designs and Patents Act 1988.

All rights reserved. No part of this book may be reproduced or utilised in any form or by any means, electronic or mechanical, including photocopying, recording or by any information storage and retrieval system, without permission in writing from JR Books.

A catalogue record for this book is available from the British Library.

Artwork © Peter Brookes

ISBN 978-1-906779-58-0

1 3 5 7 9 10 8 6 4 2

Printed in Singapore

For my *Times* colleagues

George W Bush on the campaign trail for a second term as President.

Four British citizens named as suspects in the London bombings while in Iraq US and UK forces struggle to maintain security.

An action plan is to combat anti-social behaviour through respect, a quality lacking in the relationship of Gordon Brown and Tony Blair.

President Mahmoud Ahmadinejad claims Iran has successfully enriched uranium for use in nuclear power stations.

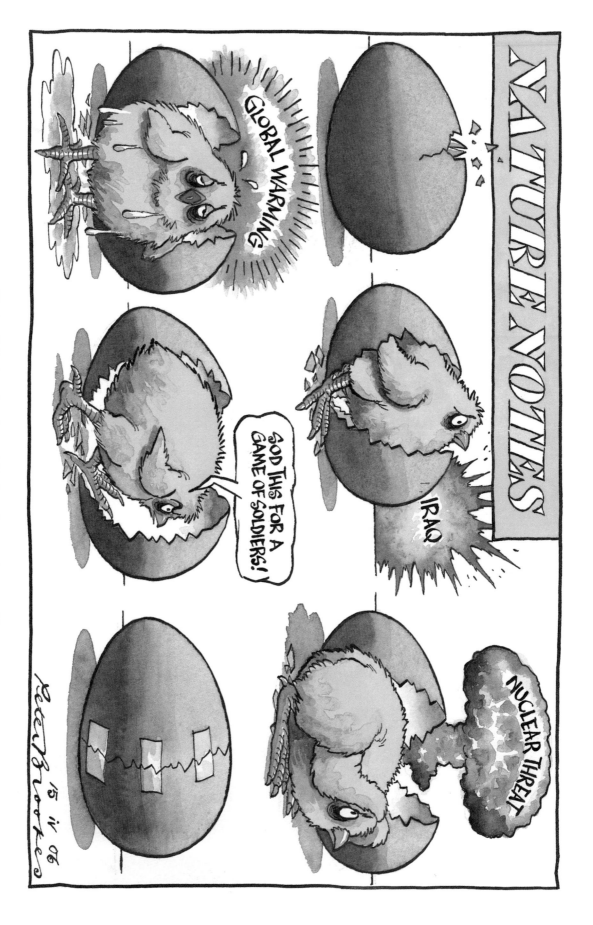

Easter fails to raise the spirits in a threatening world.

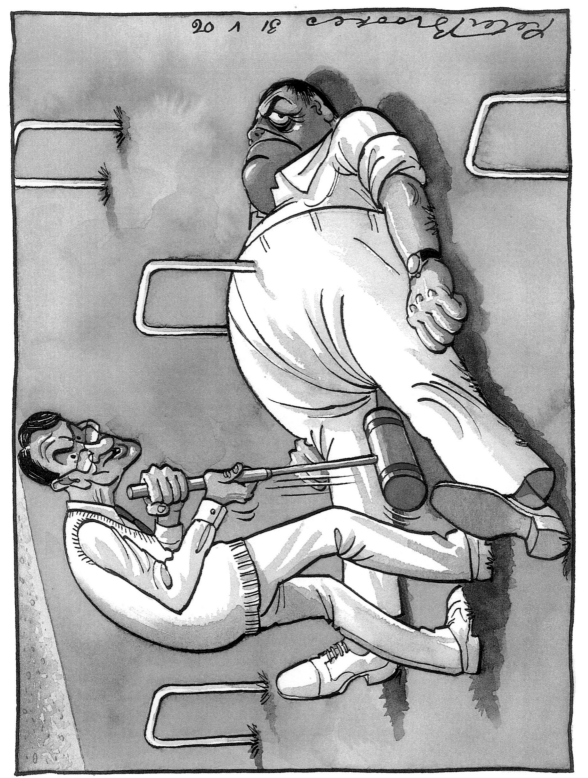

Peter Mandelson demonstrates his support after Deputy Prime Minister John Prescott is pictured playing croquet while standing in for a holidaying Tony Blair.

Having at last agreed he will step down, Tony Blair knows that in less than a year he will no longer have responsibility as Prime Minister.

SHI
CREE
OOOAAAGH!
BUSH CASSIDY
AND THE SUPINE KID
CERTIFIED
Peter Brookes
8 xii 06

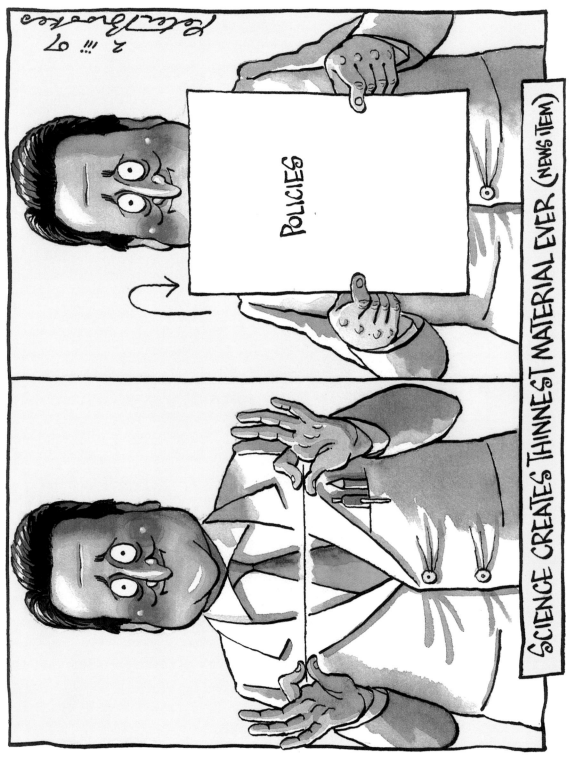

David Cameron has been leader of the opposition for more than a year without making a significant impression on the Tory party.

Tony Blair reaches his tenth anniversary as Prime Minister of Great Britain.

Tony Blair concludes his lengthy farewell tours with his legacy still dominated by the invasion of Iraq.

NATURE NOTES

Keeping the party clean

The oxpecker (*Brownbeakus artisticus*) knows its place. On the back of the massively dull grey hippo (*Gordus helpus*) scavenging for lice, ticks or fleas. And even where the sun don't shine.

7 vii 07
Peter Brookes

Gordon Brown's first cabinet includes key posts for his staunchest allies as well as Blairites.

The high cost of conflict in Iraq and Afghanistan dominates President Bush's presidency.

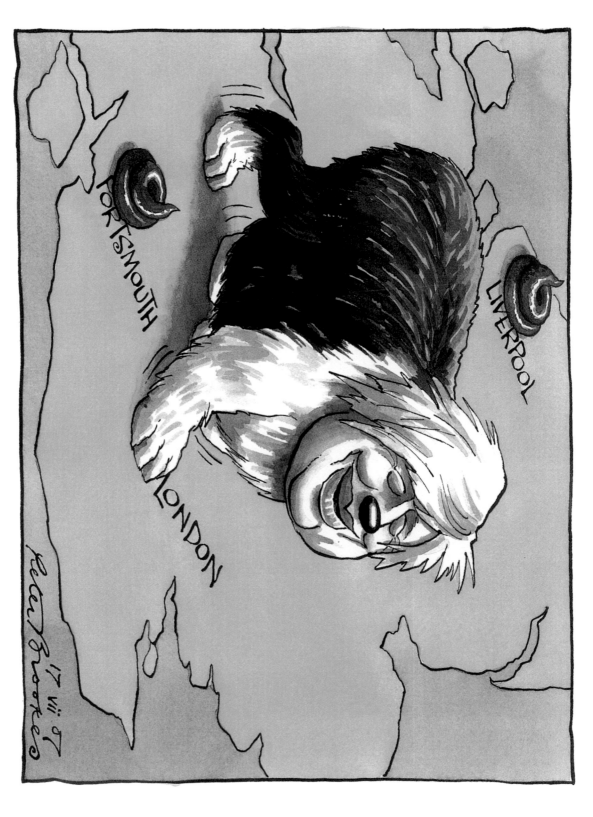

Having apologised for describing Liverpudlians as victims and Portsmouth as depressed, Boris Johnson sets his sights on London and the role of Mayor.

Cherie Blair's publishers refuse to confirm her contract could be worth as much as £1 million.

Sir Ming Campbell tells the Liberal Democrat conference the media are wrong to claim he's too old to lead.

King Abdullah makes a state visit amid protests about Saudi Arabia's human rights and arms trade record.

PEACE MISSING...

Boycotting the US-backed solution to the Middle East conflict.

Alistair Darling tries to save Northern Rock, Des Browne denies British armed forces are underfunded, Jacqui Smith recommends detention without charge for 42 days and Ruth Kelly's holiday rail engineering works overrun.

Gordon Brown uses his trip to China to discuss opportunities for British businesses more than he does human rights issues.

Bill Clinton accused of playing the race card in his wife Hillary's fight with Barack Obama.

Conservative leader David Cameron withdraws party whip from Derek Conway MP, who used public money to employ his full-time student son as a political researcher.

Archbishop of Canterbury Dr Rowan Williams says the UK will adopt aspects of Sharia law.

House of Commons Speaker Michael Martin MP faces criticism over both his handling of a review of MPs' expenses and those he had claimed for himself.

1. DRAGGING THE SPEAKER.

ARCANE TRADITIONS OF PARLIAMENT ...

26 ii 08
Peter Brookes

Violent clashes in Tibet during demonstrations in the run-up to the Beijing Olympics.

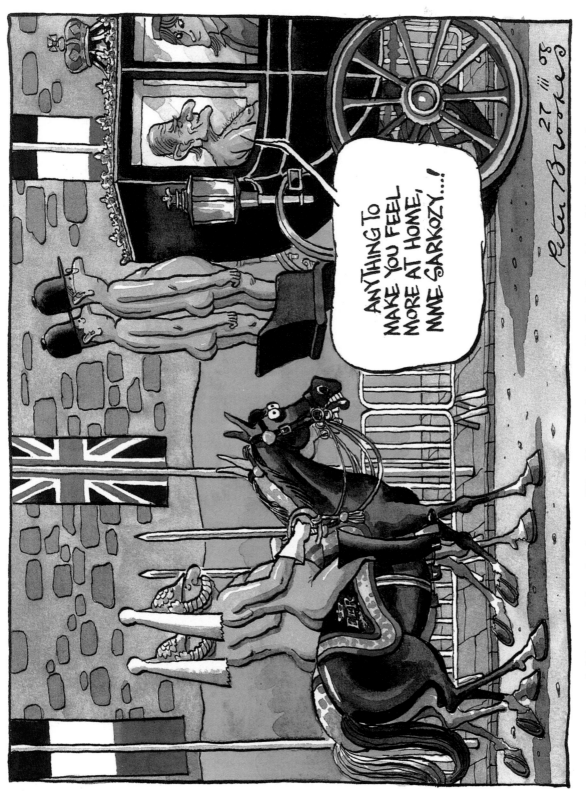

A 15-year-old nude picture of President Sarkozy's wife Carla Bruni is sold at Sotheby's during the couple's UK visit.

Initial reports suggest Morgan Tsvangirai will beat Robert Mugabe while doubts remain that the Zimbabwean President is ready to give up power.

Mugabe's Zanu-PF party beaten by the MDC, but the Presidential results have still to be declared.

NATURE NOTES

Sex Secrets of the Political Animal

Fig.1 Keeping its pecker up.

This big...

Great Shag
(Cleggoverus legoverus)

As revealed in GQ, the birdwatchers' bible, it enjoys a variety of breeding partners. Will fly upside down for a lark.

Warty Newt
(Redkenus bedkenus)

The world's first pregnant male. Fecund, but up itself.

Liberal Democrat leader Nick Clegg MP reveals he has slept with up to 30 women. While campaigning for re-election as Mayor of London, Ken Livingstone admits he has five children by three different women.

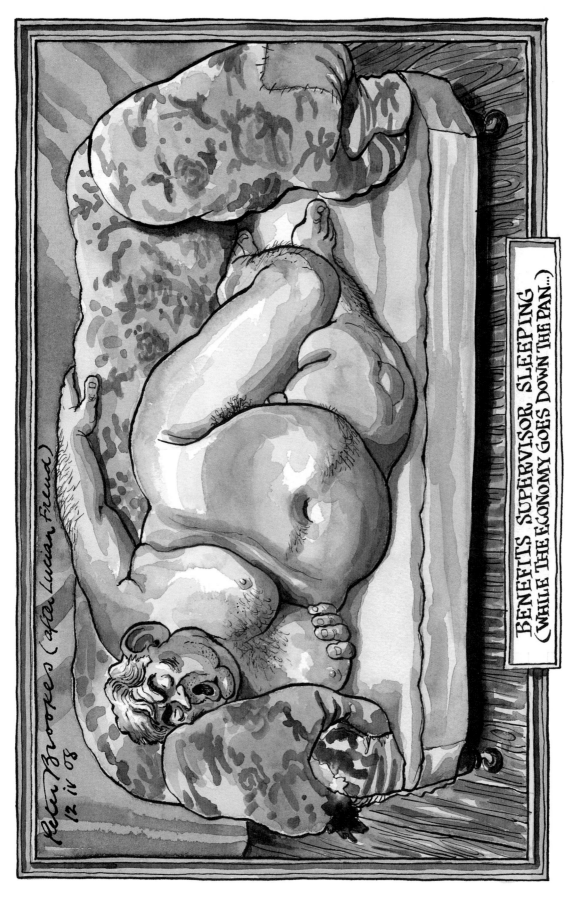

Lucian Freud's 'Benefits Supervisor Sleeping' is expected to set a record price for a work by a living artist.

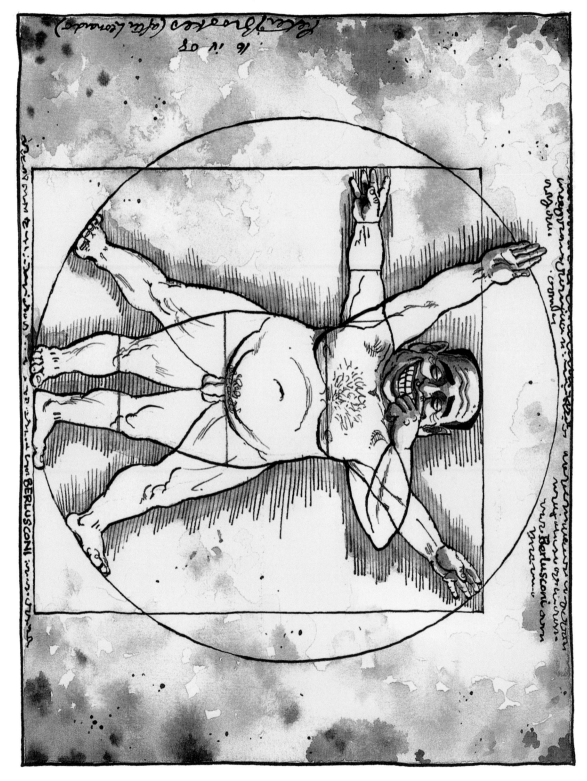

Silvio Berlusconi is again Prime Minister of Italy and moves to reassure the country's anti-immigration Northern League party.

After Josef Fritzl is arrested for the rape and 24-year imprisonment of his daughter, attention focuses on hauntingly similar cases in recent Austrian history.

Local elections see Labour's worst results in 40 years and Ken Livingstone ousted as London Mayor.

Labour's dismal performance in local polls prompts rumours that David Miliband might take over as Prime Minister.

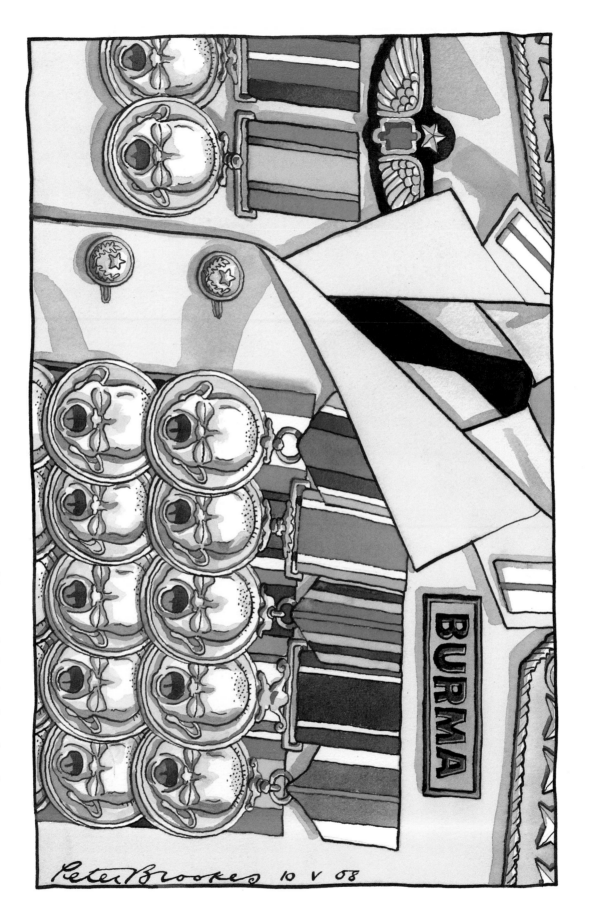

Obstructing aid for thousands of cyclone victims, the junta push on with a constitutional referendum they claim will improve democracy.

BURMA

Peter Brookes 10 V 08

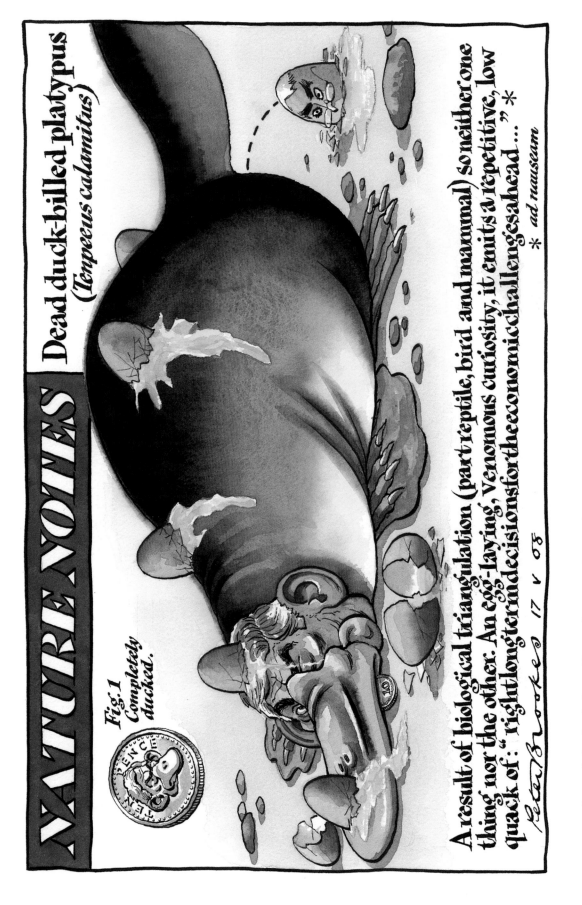

A revolt in the Labour Party threatens Brown's position as Prime Minister after the scrapping of the 10p tax band and Chancellor Alistair Darling makes hasty amends.

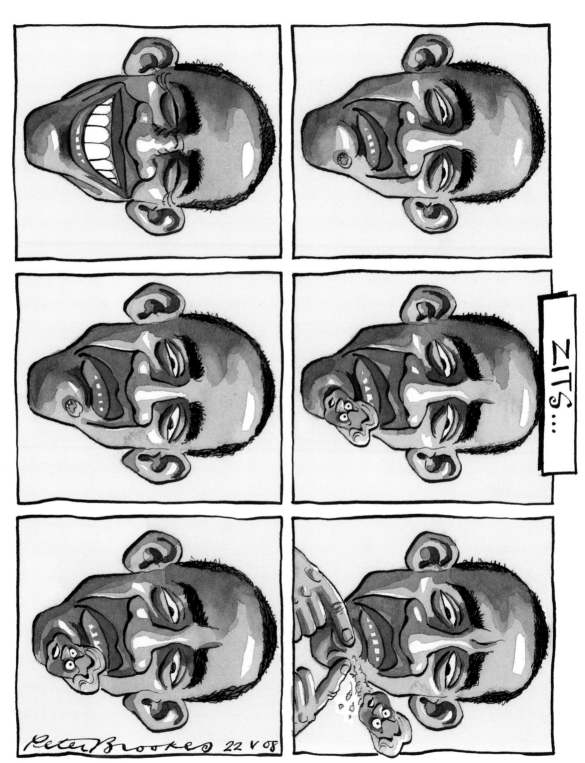

Hillary Clinton just keeps coming back in the primaries.

ZITS...

The Prime Minister is accused of snubbing the spiritual leader of Tibet in deference to China by receiving him in Lambeth Palace rather than 10 Downing Street.

Victorious Democratic candidate Obama might have faced a tough battle with Hillary Clinton but knows the fight will only get dirtier when he goes up against Senator John McCain.

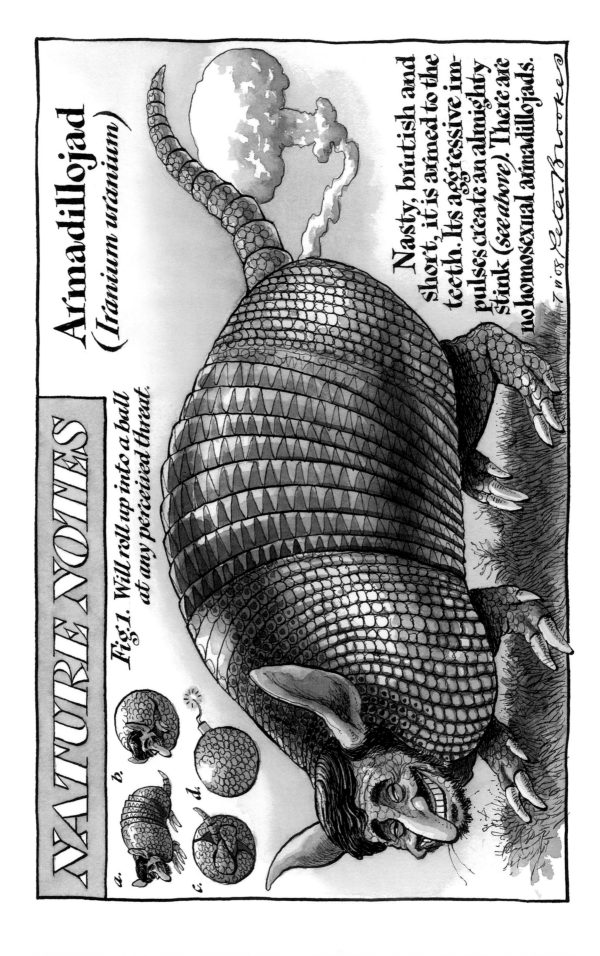

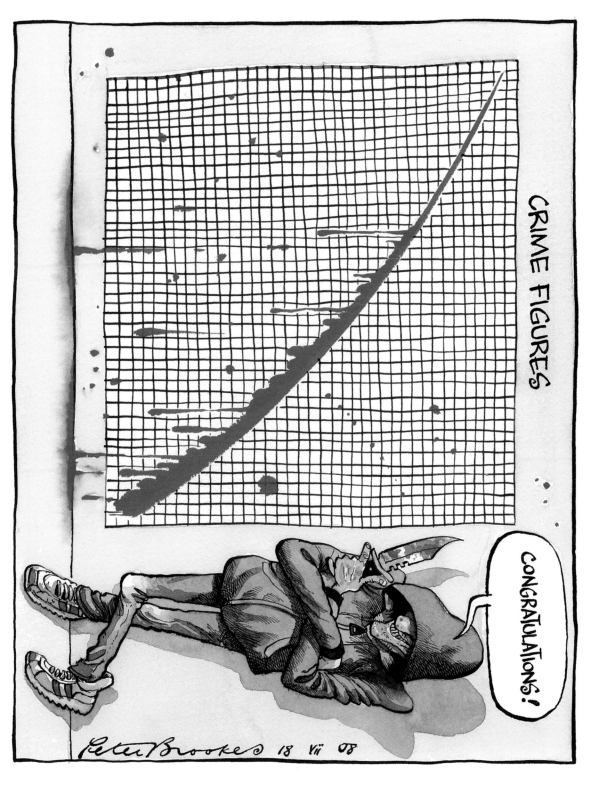

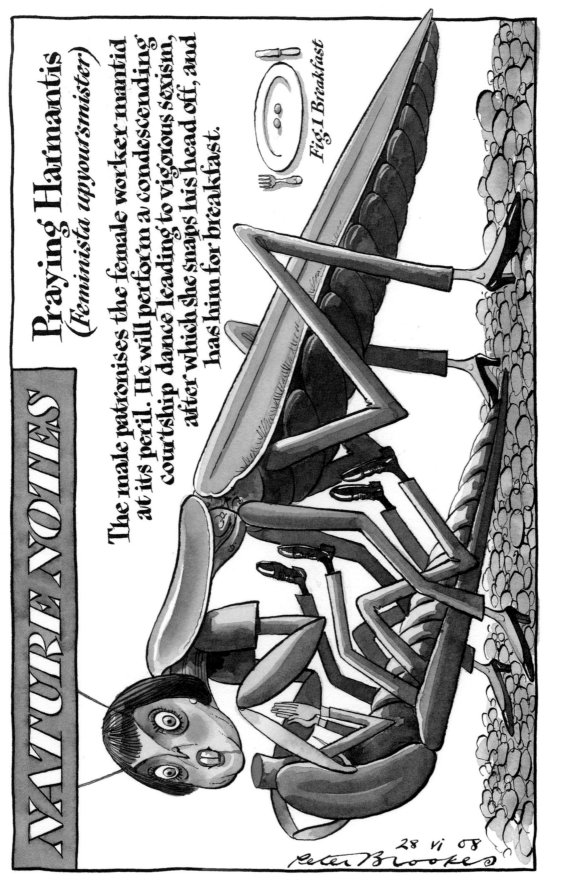

Minister for Women and Equality Harriet Harman introduces an Equalities Bill. Among its measures is the power for firms to appoint a woman over a man of the same ability.

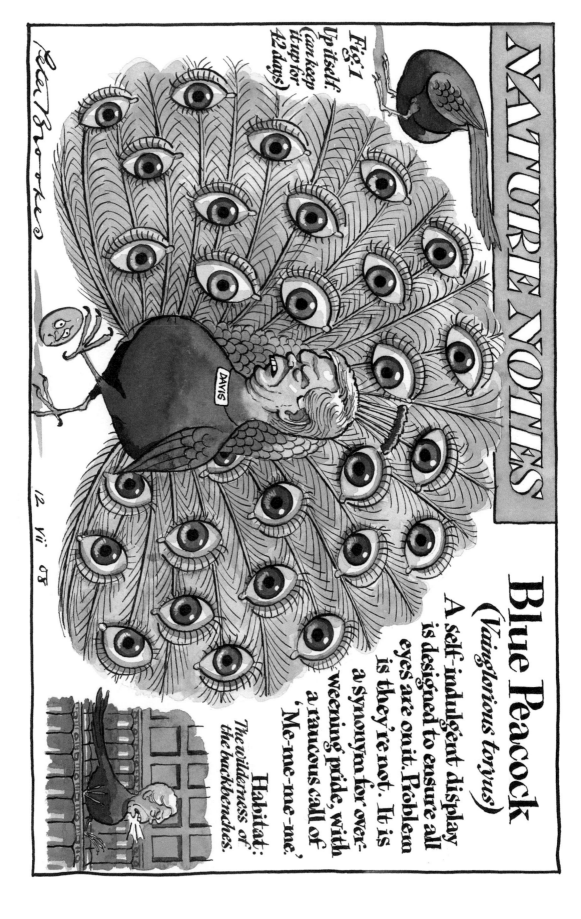

The extension of detention without charge to 42 days prompts Shadow Home Secretary David Davis to stand again as MP on the single issue of civil liberties.

The safe Labour seat of Glasgow East is lost in a humiliating by-election defeat to the Scottish National Party.

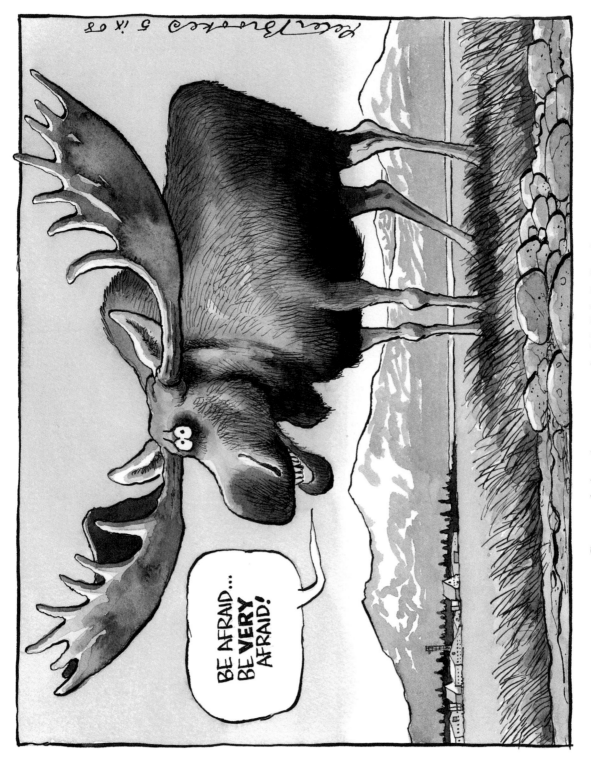

Contemplating the prospect of a McCain/Palin victory.

Gordon Brown combats the deepening global financial crisis.

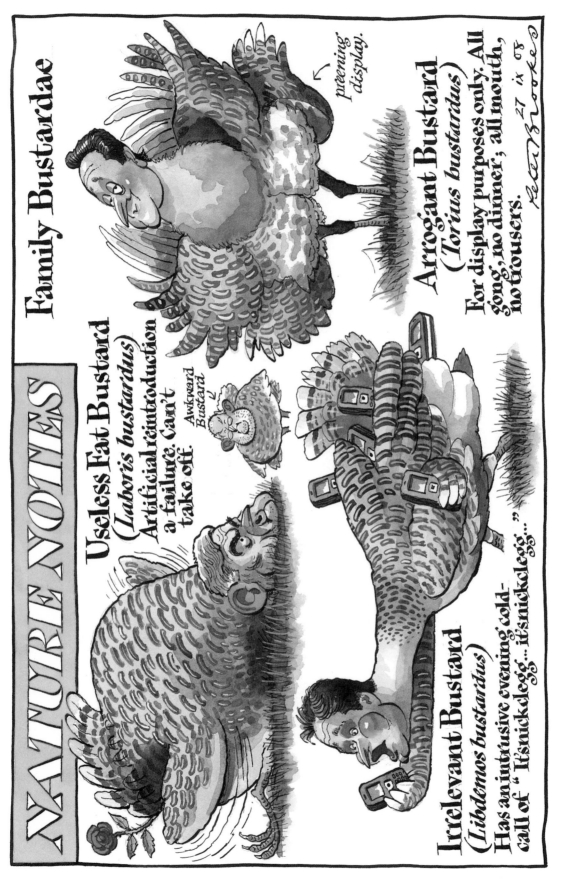

Former Home Secretary Charles Clarke warns Brown has just months to turn Labour's fortunes around. A computerised calling system delivers a message from the Liberal Democrat leader to 250,000 lucky voters.

One of Alistair Darling's Tory predecessors, Norman Lamont, had attained notoriety for apparently singing in the bath on Britain's exit from the ERM.

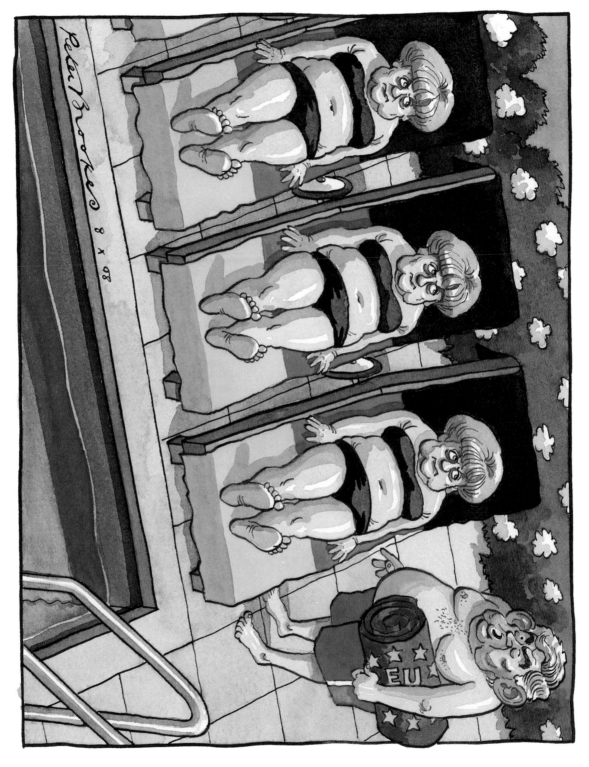

Chancellor Angela Merkel takes centre stage as it emerges that Germany has no plans to introduce legislation to protect savings from the financial crisis.

Shadow Chancellor George Osborne faces allegations that he solicited a donation from Russian billionaire Oleg Deripaska.

In the depths of world-wide financial calamity, Gordon Brown manages to avoid personal disaster.

Jonathan Ross is suspended without pay after controversial phone calls he and Russell Brand have made to Andrew Sachs.

The new American President elect – Barack Hussein Obama.

As unemployment reaches its highest level since 1997 Prince Charles prepares to celebrate his 60th birthday with no sign of a vacancy at the top.

(after 'Washington Crossing the Delaware')

'The Death of New Labour' Peter Brookes after Damien Hirst 25 xi 08

Even fewer will be able to afford Damien Hirst prices as Alistair Darling's pre-budget report recommends a 45p tax band for earnings above £150,000.

Serjeant at Arms Jill Pay and Speaker Michael Martin share criticism for not preventing the police raid on Damian Green MP's Parliamentary office.

Gordon Brown may think he's saving the world, but Germany's finance minister strongly criticises his policies.

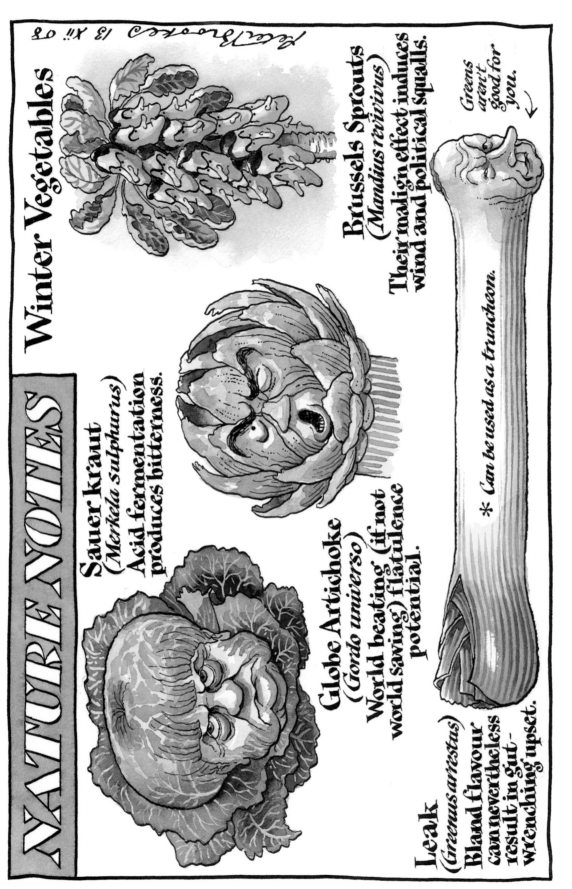

NATURE NOTES

Winter Vegetables

Sauer kraut
(Merkela sulphurus)
Acid fermentation produces bitterness.

Globe Artichoke
(Gordo universo)
World beating (if not world saving) flatulence potential.

Leak
(Greenus arrestus)
Bland flavour can nevertheless result in gut-wrenching upset.

Brussels Sprouts
(Mandius revivirus)
Their malign effect induces wind and political squalls.

Greens aren't good for you.

* Can be used as a truncheon.

RedBrooks 13 xii 08

Damian Green MP is arrested in connection with leaks from the Home Office. Germany's Angela Merkel falls out with her finance minister by backing Gordon Brown's financial leadership.

Iraqi journalist Muntadar al-Zaidi bids farewell to out-going President Bush on his last visit to the region.

Sarah Palin's high profile as Republican Vice President candidate fuelled speculation that the Alaskan hunting enthusiast would run for the top job in 2012.

The end nears for President Bush's term in power.

Twinkle, twinkle, little star,
How I wonder what you are!
White with phosphorescent glow,
Burning children down below.

16 i 09

Peter Brookes

Israel denies claims that it used white phosphorus shells – internationally banned from civilian areas – in its assault on Gaza.

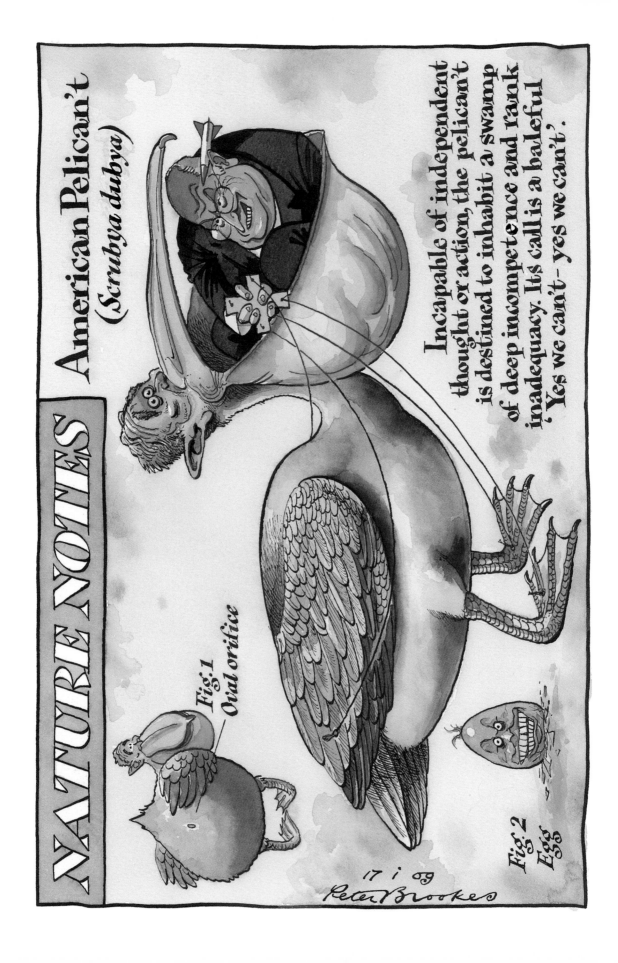

20 i 09
Peter Brookes

President Obama signals the closure of Guantanamo Bay and outlaws controversial interrogation techniques such as waterboarding.

NATURE NOTES

Fig:1 Hitting the ground flying:

Yes Toucan
(Obama whatacharma)

It carries before its slender frame the heavy burden of world expectation, raising some doubts that the whole construct can fly (see Fig:1). Phooey. A much more optimistic appraisal can be found in *The Audacity of Hoopoes, Totalbollocks Press, Yale*, and *Dreams from My Feather, Penguin Books*.

Barack Obama attains rock star levels of popularity as the new President and author of *The Audacity of Hope* and *Dreams from my Father*.

Ailing financial institutions retain vast amounts of public cash as Carol Thatcher is dropped from BBC's *The One Show* after refusing to apologise for saying 'golliwog' in an off-air comment about a black tennis player.

Charles Darwin celebrates his 200th birthday.

Home Secretary Jacqui Smith to face inquiry over nominating her sister's London house as her main home and claiming second-home expenses on her constituency residence.

Royal Bank of Scotland's 2008 losses of £24.1 billion are the biggest in British history and it requires a further £13 billion in aid.

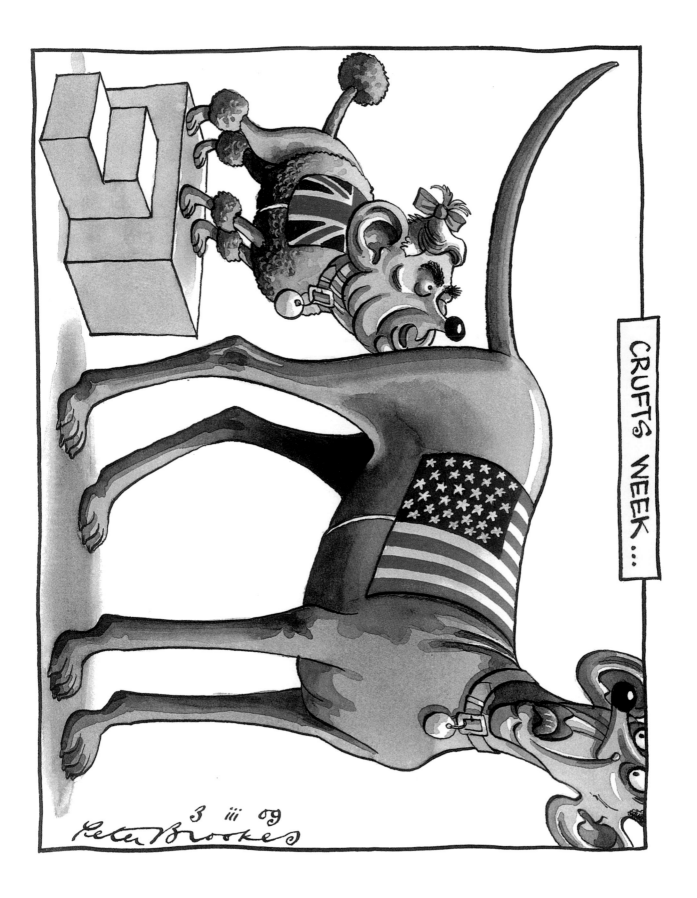

CRUFTS WEEK...

3 iii 09
Peter Brookes

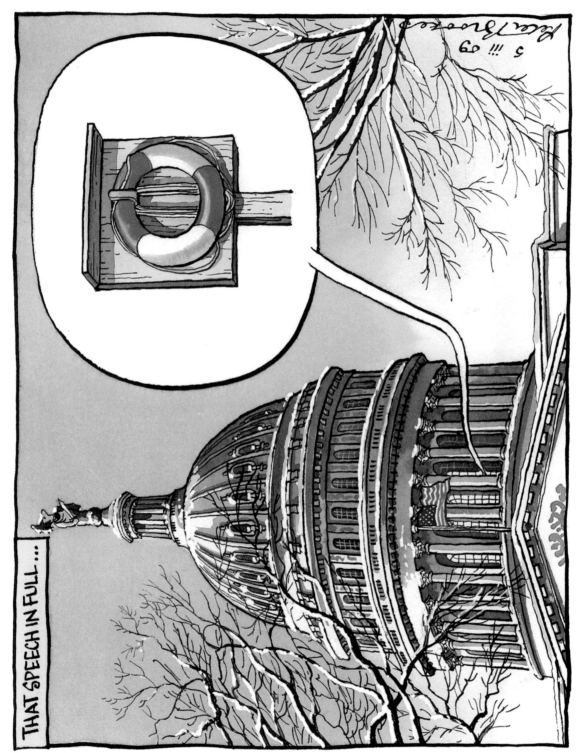

Gordon Brown hopes his speech to the US Congress will aid his sinking domestic reputation.

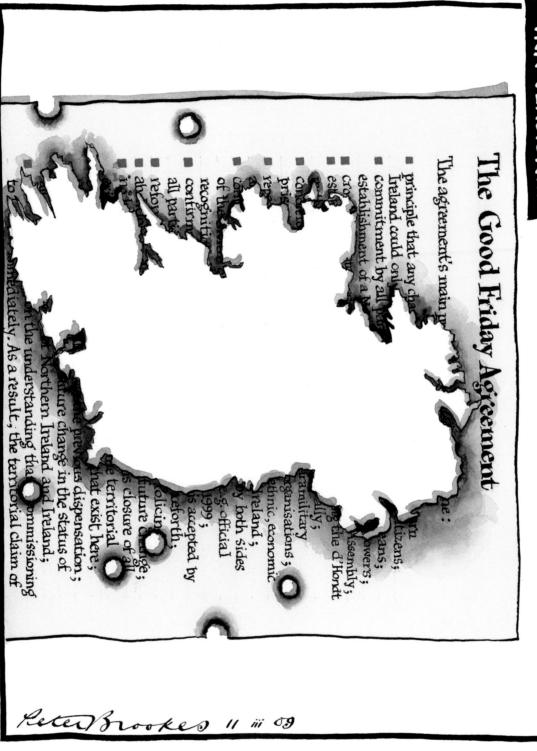

IRA VERSION...

The Good Friday Agreement

The agreement's main p...

principle that any cha...
Ireland could onl...
commitment by all part...
establishment of a N...
cro...
est...
...

...recogniti...
...confirm...
...all part...
...refo...
...

...rotary;
...organisations;
...thnic, economic...
...reland;
...y both sides
...e.g. official
...1999;
...is accepted by
...eforth.
...Assembly;
...g the d'Hondt

...ne previous dispensation;
...ure change in the status of
...r Northern Ireland and Ireland;
...n the understanding tha
...ommissioning
...immediately. As a result, the territorial claim of
...to...
...future change;
...s closure of all
...e territorial
...hat exist here;
...olicin

Peter Brookes 11 iii 09

The Continuity IRA claim responsibility for the murder of a policeman in Northern Ireland, just days after killing two British soldiers.

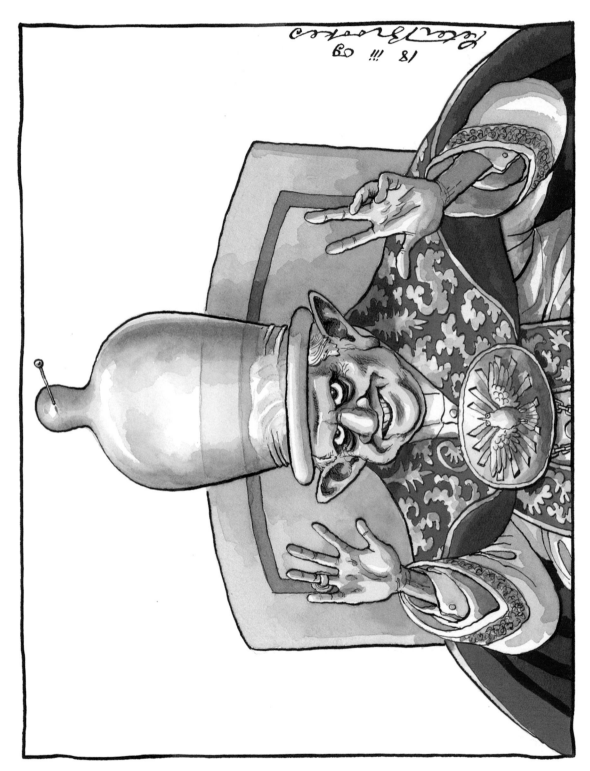

The Pope uses his first trip to Africa to say that condoms are not the answer to the continent's HIV/Aids epidemic.

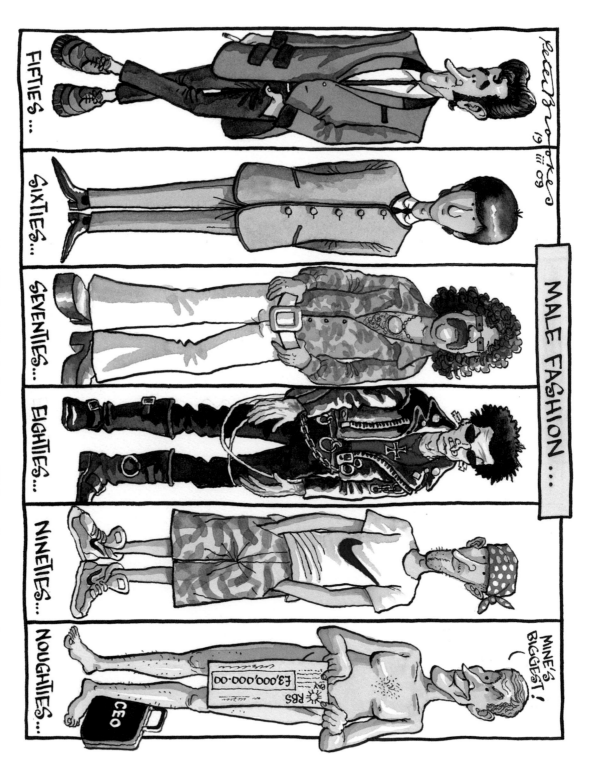

Even fuller details of Sir Fred Goodwin's generous RBS pension are exposed.

Some regret Ken Clarke striding back to the front bench in his beloved Hush Puppies after he unilaterally downgrades the Conservative promise to cut inheritance tax to the status of aspiration.

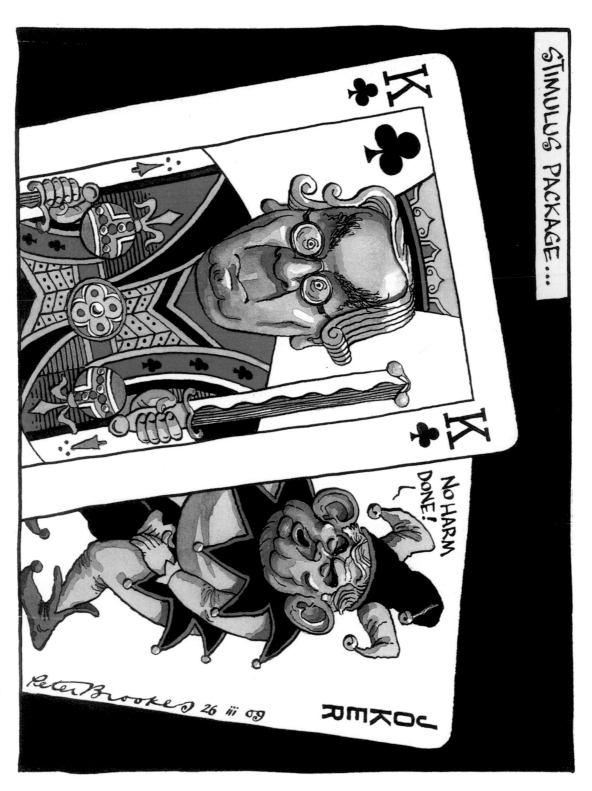

Bank of England governor Mervyn King warns Gordon Brown that the country can't afford another big fiscal stimulus.

President Obama commits more troops to Afghanistan to create stability in the country.

The US President attends the emergency G20 summit on the international financial crisis hosted by London and judged to be a success.

THE FUTILITY OF HOPE...

2 iv 09
Peter Brookes

BARACK
OBAMA
gave Gordon Brown
reason to live here
April
2009
⌗

President Obama and President Sarkozy of France hail a new era of cooperation.

Evidence grows of excessive police force at the G20 as Gordon Brown adviser Damian McBride quits after planning Tory email smear campaign.

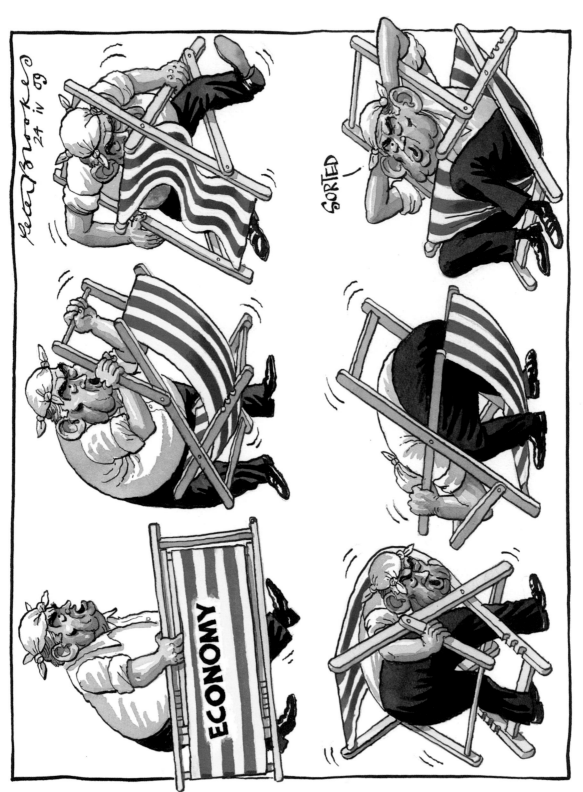

A sunny spring approaches with many radical measures taken by the Prime Minister to combat the country's deep recession.

The UK's first cases of the swine flu that originated in Mexico are confirmed in Scotland as fears of a global pandemic grow.

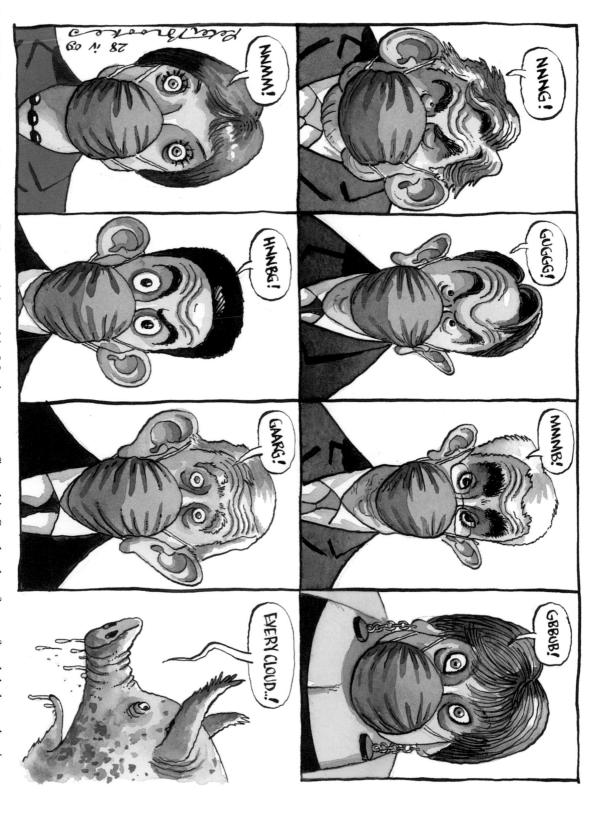

NATURE NOTES

Gastropads
How the upper and lower orders of molluscs maximise their living arrangements.

Fig.1 *Gastropadus taxpayerus vulgaris*   Fig.2 *Gastropada cabinetminista*

MPs' expenses come under daily scrutiny, including those of communities secretary Hazel Blears, who has claimed on three properties in one year.

The expenses revelations threatening to overwhelm the Commons show MPs claims include tampons and horse manure.

The role of Speaker Michael Martin in handling MPs' expenses is heavily criticised.

GLASGOW KISS....

Michael Martin, MP for Glasgow North East, finally agrees to overwhelming pressure from his fellow parliamentarians to step down as Speaker.

Burma's pro-democracy leader Aung San Suu Kyi faces trial for violating house arrest after an American man pays her an uninvited visit.

Fresh revelations in the MP expenses scandal soap opera include details about couples including Julie Kirkbride and Andrew MacKay.

Britain's Got Talent favourite Susan Boyle makes it through to the final (and loses).

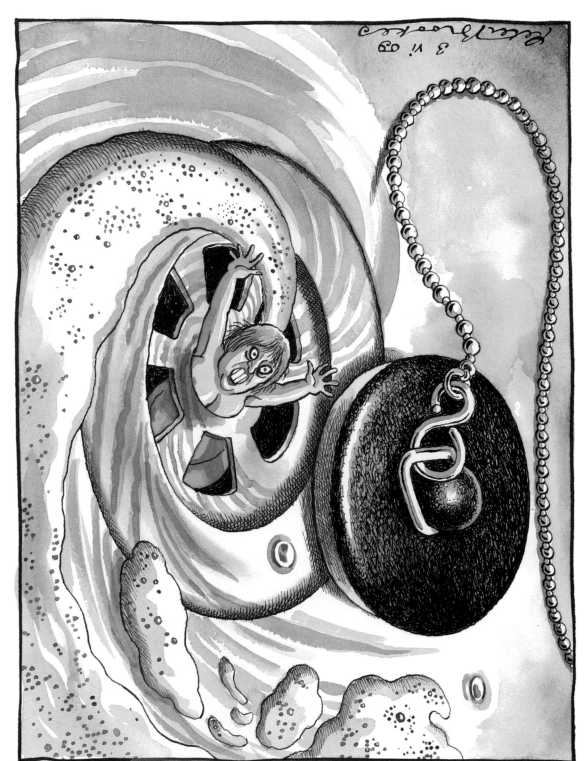

Jacqui Smith, whose expenses claims came in for criticism and included a bath plug, resigns as Home Secretary while Gordon Brown reshuffles his cabinet.

THE GREAT ESCAPE ...

Communities Secretary and motorcyclist Hazel Blears announces her great escape from Gordon Brown's cabinet just as the country is about to vote in local and European elections.

USA

MIDDLE EAST

On President Obama's first visit to Egypt he is to make a highly anticipated speech on the course of his new administration's relations with the Muslim world.

Peter Brookes 5 vi 09

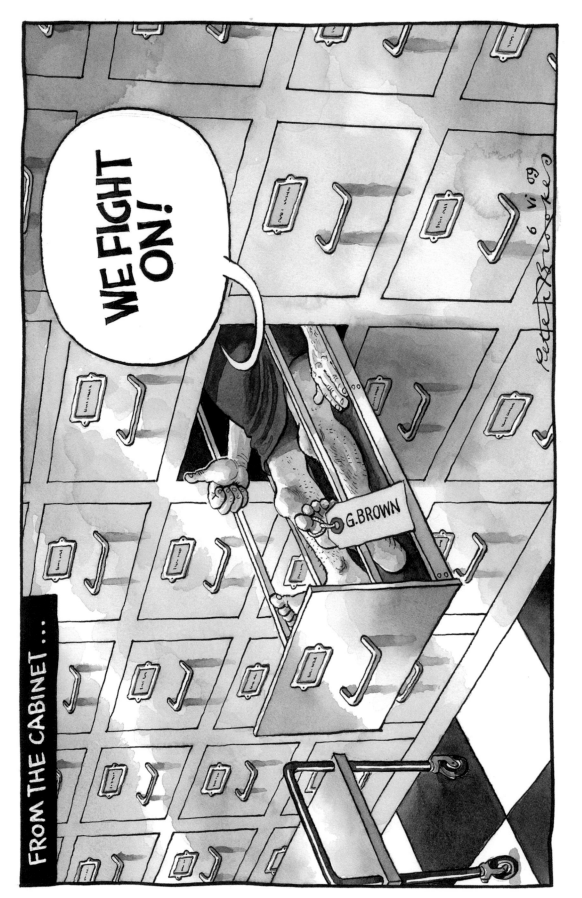

Gordon Brown suffers huge election defeats and the resignation of a number of senior ministers from his cabinet.

The full horror of the European and local election wipeout sinks in.

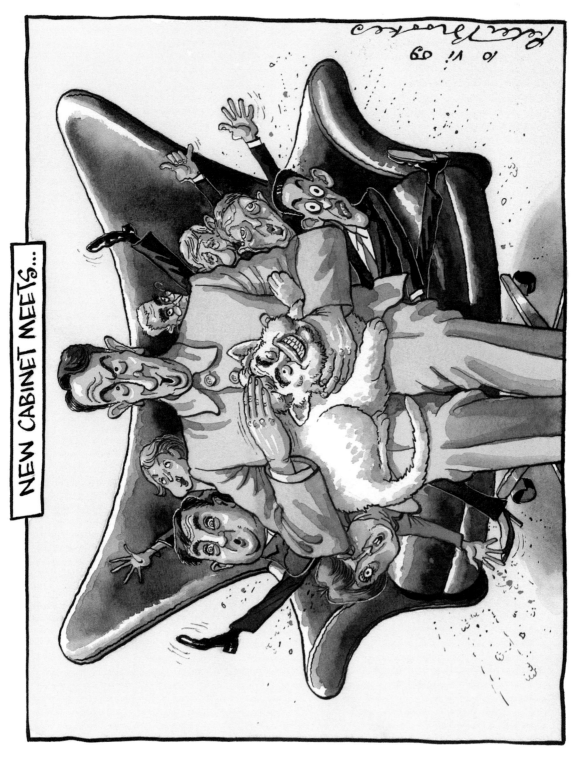

NEW CABINET MEETS...

Peter Mandelson plays a key part in supporting the weakened Gordon Brown against leadership challenges after the election rout.

Manchester United's Cristiano Ronaldo transfers to Real Madrid for a record £80 million.

Violence during the Iranian electoral dispute between President Mahmoud Ahmadinejad and opposition leader Hossein Mousavi is reported via the internet amid media censorship.

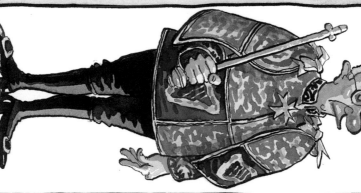

Peter Brookes 19 vi 09

GREAT OFFICES OF STATE & PARLIAMENT...

SILVER STICK

PURSUIVANT OF ARMS

BLACK ROD

BLACK REDACTOR

After weeks of leaks, MPs expenses are finally published – with the most important information blacked out.

Iraq marks the day that US troops pull out its towns and cities and return to their bases.